How One Woman's Life Changed When God Exchanged His Beauty for Her Ashes

*By
Dr. Ashlei N. Evans*

Copyright © 2019 Ashlei N. Evans

To contact the author visit: www.theashexchange.com

All rights reserved. This book or any portion thereof may not be reproduced or used in any manner whatsoever without the express written permission of the author except for the use of brief quotations in a book review.

> Scripture quotations identified as "AMP" are from the Amplified® Bible, Copyright © 1954, 1958, 1962, 1964, 1965, 1987 by The Lockman Foundation Used by permission." (www.Lockman.org).
>
> Scripture quotations identified as "ESV" are from the ESV® Bible (The Holy Bible, English Standard Version®), copyright © 2001 by Crossway, a publishing ministry of Good News Publishers. Used by permission. All rights reserved.
>
> Scripture quotations identified as "NIV" are from THE HOLY BIBLE, NEW INTERNATIONAL VERSION®, NIV® Copyright © 1973, 1978, 1984, 2011 by Biblica, Inc.® Used by permission. All rights reserved worldwide.
>
> Scripture quotations identified as "NKJV" from the New King James Version ®. Copyright © 1982 by Thomas Nelson, Inc. Used by permission. All rights reserved.
>
> Scripture quotations identified as "NLT" are taken from the *Holy Bible*, New Living Translation, copyright © 1996, 2004, 2015 by Tyndale House Foundation. Used by permission of Tyndale House Publishers, Inc., Carol Stream, Illinois 60188. All rights reserved.

Logo Design: Derek J. Murphy Enterprises

Photo by © Andrea Pa Photography

Dedication

Ashes…Individually its particles are light, but together they become heavy burdens filling our insides with darkness. As we receive His love, we're filled with His light exposing us to the image of God that was implanted in us. At that moment, our ashes are exchanged for the beauty God created within.

May this book impart wisdom and knowledge into the lives of young women who struggle with understanding who they are in Christ. This book is compiled with personal testimonies, poetic reflections, and scriptural references to reflect my journey to finding myself in Christ and walking with Him.

"To all who mourn in Israel, he will give a crown of beauty for ashes, a joyous blessing instead of mourning, festive praise instead of despair. In their righteousness, they will be like great oaks that the LORD has planted for his own glory."

Isaiah 61:3 NLT

Table of Contents

Foreword by Dr. J.T. Flowers

Introduction 1

Chapter 1: In The Beginning 3

Chapter 2: Living a Reality with No Truth 17

Chapter 3: Learning to Love and Be Loved 23

Chapter 4: Reason for Being 35

Chapter 5: Trusting the Position and the Process 47

Chapter 6: Running the Race 55

Chapter 7: Living a Consecrated Life 61

Closing 67

Foreword by Dr. J.T. Flowers

Every life is a story filled with many chapters; some chapters are filled with wonderful successes, others are filled with great pain, suffering and disappointments. Every life is filled with problems, strengths, imperfections and of course, weaknesses. God created us relational beings, and it is within the confines of so many powerful relationships that God uses people to elevate the quality of life for so many as we share our stories, openly and honestly.

There are no perfect people on planet earth. This world is filled with many hurting people who desperately need to know how to rise above dysfunction, abuse, the hurts and disappointments of the past, and the turbulence of soul unique to living in a fallen world. Indeed, amid the pain and suffering, God has a wonderful plan for the lives of all those who are willing to simply entrust their lives to Him. What a "Divine Exchange"! God takes our shattered lives and shapes us into vessels of honor fit for the Master's good use.

In her book, "The Ash Exchange," Dr. Ashlei N. Evans shares insight into how God, our Sovereign Creator, takes a "torn life" and creates a "triumphant masterpiece". God is no respecter of persons! What He has done in her life, He can and will do for all those who cry out to Him. May your life be transformed forever after reading this powerfully transparent writing of Dr. Ashlei N. Evans. You will be captivated and challenged, even as I was at the reading of her story. God alone heals the wounded soul. Blessings!

Introduction

For years, I've dreamed of writing a book. I started one year ago and stopped. The purpose was there, but as I began to outline the chapters, I realized there was a message within me that God desired me to deliver. The only thing is, the message was still being finalized. I am aware no one is perfect, but I do believe there is a season and time for everything to be done. There was still much healing that needed to take place before I could truly pour out to others. I was in a place where I was on fire for the Lord and very active in the church, but I needed an encounter with God that would position me to know God for myself.

One day in February of 2018, during my prayer time, I clearly heard the Lord tell me to begin writing my story. He reminded me of Revelations 12 which states,

And they overcame and conquered him because of the blood of the Lamb and because of the word of their testimony, for they did not love their life and renounce their faith even when faced with death.
Revelation 12:11 NLT

This scripture brings awareness to the power a story has to encourage and transform the lives of others. I've never been one for attention, but a few days prior to this revelation I was asked to share my testimony to a group of inner city girls in middle school and high school. As much as I write about the love of God, I felt the need to also express exactly what God has done for me. I must admit the idea made me nervous, but as I accepted the invitation there was a sense of peace.

Transparency is the one area many believers struggle to offer due to all the religious and legalistic protocols, but transparency is necessary for people to truly know their freedom is available. My journey in life hasn't been perfect, nevertheless God continues to move in and through me despite my moments of failure. My prayer is that this book would set you free and soften your heart to receive God's love. No matter how far you drift away from God, remember there is nothing that can keep us away from His love.

1

In The Beginning

*But the way of the wicked is like deep darkness;
they do not know what makes them stumble.
Proverbs 4:19 ESV*

Behind the smiles there lived a child who wept silent tears for years
Birthed into a world of dysfunction
She never quite understood why her existence was so unique
"Why me?" was the story of her life and the depression consumed her
Darkness began to reside within and her soul started to deteriorate causing her to slowly but surely exist in a state of ashes.
Burned by so many situations, she stopped seeing the beauty that resided in her.
It wasn't until she heard from God, through Isaiah, that she began to embrace the fact that all that was before was not an accident, but a process.

American by birth but Nigerian by blood is how I typically describe myself nowadays thanks to AncestryDNA. For the sake of simplifying my background, I'll focus on my life in the great nation of America! I was born and raised in Houston, Texas on June 16, 1987 at 6:55pm to be exact. My parents, Vicki Teresa Gordon and Freddie Evans Sr., were married more than once which, in my eyes, makes my existence all the more special. I was my mother's only child and my father's fourth child. Being my father's one and only daughter, he tried to continue his tradition of having his children named after him. My oldest brother Enoch Frederick, whom I've never met, my second oldest brother Fred, and my third brother Freddie were all unfortunately named after my father. So he attempted to name me Fredricka, but thankfully my mother was strong-willed enough to simply just say NO! They considered Kimberly but eventually Ashlei, supposedly taken from Young and the Restless, earned the privilege of being my name.

My childhood was great for the most part. I was active in karate, ballet, and I was very sociable. I was a member of St. Agnes Baptist Church, and my father and I were baptized on the same day there, June 7, 1992. Life was what every kid would dream of living until it all came to an end with my father leaving. I was around 7 years old and I was sleeping on the couch in the living room. I woke up to the chaotic sounds of my mother and father fighting. I didn't know what to do, so I laid there holding a pillow over my head. The arguing grew loud and all of a sudden I saw my father burst through the doors of their room with my mother trailing behind him. My mother sat down, and my father remained standing. He put his hand out and told me to come with him. As I remember that moment, I believe it was one of the most pivotal decisions I had ever made. I loved my mother and father, but, with no hesitation, I jumped up and ran into my mother's arms. I had never had to choose between my mother and father before, but the reason why I made this choice will later be revealed. My father's face of anger transformed into a picture of defeat. He left that day, leaving my life forever changed.

My father leaving catapulted a series of misfortunate events. Shortly after his disappearance, I found out my mother had been keeping a secret. I remember one day she sat on the couch with one of my cousins. My other cousin and I watched from the 2nd floor balcony. She then pulled out a bag of hair and removed her wig. My cousin sitting next to her was too young to really process what had just been revealed, so she laughed. I was not informed enough to understand what was happening, so I was emotionless. The significance of her being sick hadn't dawned on me until things began to change at an accelerated pace.

As a result of my father leaving, my mother now had to downsize. Being a kid, I wasn't included in all the discussions, but I do remember collecting boxes from my mom's friend's house on different occasions. Shortly after those visits, we were moving into a new house. It was smaller and the neighborhood looked older. I had to go to a new school that was less affluent and more diverse. Transition did not bother me because being with my mother assured me that everything was going to be okay.

After my dad left we went to a few churches, but my mother spent most of her time at Success in Christ Higher Dimension Christian Center. We spent many long nights there shouting, singing, and hearing the pastor preach. My little cousins would join me sometimes and they would fall asleep on the pew having been there so long. I truly believe that's what helped her stay hopeful.

She never showed she was struggling. She never cried in front of me, but there was one night that really showed me just how sick she was. I heard her coughing and I got up only to see her bent over her sink. That moment filled my heart with grief. I had never seen my mother in that much pain. Seeing her struggle made me endeavor to not complain and try to help her however I could. I remember my grandmother and my mom's siblings would often visit to assist. Due to my desire to not add to her problems, I began to internalize my thoughts and feelings. Unfortunately, this also led to me struggling to express myself.

Daddy's Gone

I don't recall seeing my father visit us in our new house. He did call one time, and even as a child I understood the disrespect he showed. He had moved to Louisiana with his mistress, someone he supposedly met through his cousin. He was living with her and her 3 children. He had also taken one of my half-brothers with him. My mother spoke on the phone with my father first, and then she handed the phone to me. My father spoke briefly with me and then passed the phone to the mistress. Soon he had me calling all these other people all these nicknames as if they were my family. At the time, I just said it to get off the phone. I just couldn't understand how a man who left his daughter and wife could possibly call me and have me talking to the other woman and her kids.

When I got older, I realized my father was operating out of a pattern. About a year prior to my parents separating, my mother was in her restroom doing her makeup and she pulled me to her side and said, "You know you have another brother right?" Up until then, I had only known of the brother who lived with us. We didn't share the same mom, but he was always around. My mother said my brother was from my father's previous marriage and he was two years older. At the time I was 8, so this news was definitely a shock to me. Shortly after she revealed this news to me, I was riding in my dad's truck to meet my brother for the first time. Considering my brother was an athlete, my dad took us to a field where they threw the football with each other. I knew early on that was not my calling so I stepped back and watched. I never felt any jealously towards my father's relationship with my brothers. In fact, I always enjoyed seeing them connect. When I would see my father interact with them, it was apparent he loved them dearly. He loved us all, but he never knew how to love us beyond being a provider.

The Assault

I don't remember exactly when it began, but I know it was after my father left. My mother would often watch my cousins and because she was often weak she would rest in her room. I remember one time we were playing hide-and-go-seek. My oldest cousin seemed to make the rules and he specifically put me on his team. I never enjoyed being around him, but I was forced to be his partner. He pulled me in my bedroom and forced me to lay on my back. He pulled down his pants and forced me to perform oral sex on him. It was the most disgusting feeling I ever had, but he was stronger and wouldn't allow me to get up. I felt myself choking while tears streamed down my eyes, and then he ejaculated leaving semen on my shirt. Nothing was said. He just got up and joined the rest of the cousins as if the game was still being played. The abuse continued over a period of time as he became more and more bold forcing himself inside of me, even at my grandmother's house.

I never said a word about it to anyone because soon the day came - my mother passed away. I know she would have done everything in her power to keep me safe, but I couldn't bare telling her what happened considering my father had left and she had cancer. Even after my mother died, my cousin continued to abuse me. It finally stopped when I entered into middle school, and it was only a result of my menstrual cycle arriving. For some, starting your period is the worst thing ever, but for me it was my saving grace. I had overheard being on your cycle meant you could have children. When my cousin came to abuse me once again, I told him I started my period and that was the end of it. Although he never touched me again, I was left with scars.

Goodbye and Hello

It was October 1996 and I was riding in the car with my uncle. He said we were going to visit my mother in the hospital. I didn't like the idea of hospitals because 4 months prior my mother's father had passed away. There was a fear within me that I would get to the hospital and see her in a condition that would solidify the thoughts that haunted me. We arrived at the hospital and took the elevator to her floor.

We walked to the door and my uncle knocked. My grandmother opened the door and whispered something to my uncle who followed behind her. I was told to wait for a minute. After a few minutes, my grandmother opened the door and I looked at my mom who appeared to be sleeping peacefully. The only thing was, she wasn't breathing. I didn't cry right away. I was numb. My grandmother told me that the last thing my mother said to her was she loved me and she didn't want me to live with my father. I walked to the other side of the bed and sat on the couch next to my grandmother. The nurse walked in looked at me and said, "You must be Vicki's baby girl. She talked about you all the time." Then, she pointed to some pictures I had drawn which were posted on my mom's bulletin board.

I didn't play a role in planning the funeral, but I remember driving to the church in the limousine. When I arrived, there were many friends and family members, but the one person who wasn't there was my father. By that time, I had allowed myself to believe I had no father. Similar to the phrase, "out of sight out of mind" he wasn't there, so I didn't think of him. At one point in the funeral, the pastor officiating the ceremony asked me to stand next to her. I honestly don't recall everything she said, but I know she spoke life over me.

A few weeks after the funeral, the custody battle began. I had resumed going back to school and one day I was called to the office to go home early. It took me by surprise because my grandmother hadn't said anything to me about leaving school. I packed my things up and walked to the front desk only to see my father and an unfamiliar face. I struggled to hug my father because he had become a stranger to me. He introduced the unfamiliar face who happened to be the woman he was living with. He said he was taking me home. I had a very uneasy feeling about it. I got in the truck and sat in the backseat. I asked where we were going and he stated we were going to Louisiana. Thoughts began to flood my mind and I started asking if my grandmother knew and if she would be coming to get me. After so many questions with no answer, I stared out the window and started to cry.

Eventually, I cried myself to sleep and awakened to the whispers of my father. He said I had been brainwashed and there were probably cops at the house ready to arrest him. Eventually we arrived in Leesville, LA where he was living with his mistress and her three kids. She had two girls and one boy who was close to my age. There were bunk beds and I was told I would sleep on the bottom one. I greeted everyone and asked to speak with my grandmother. Finally, my father put her on the phone. My grandmother was frantic and my aunt was with her. They asked me if I was okay and where I was. The only thing I could tell them was I was in Louisiana. I cried just speaking to them thinking I may never see them again. They said I would come home soon. My father then informed me he would be getting me some clothes and enrolling me into school there. I think I was in school for about a week. I felt like a foreigner and I didn't really know how to explain my predicament to students or teachers. I just stayed to myself and didn't talk much. One day after returning from school, my dad said he had to take me back to Houston for a court hearing. I said ok, but inside I was relieved. Finally, I would be free!!!

Home Again

I met my grandmother at the courthouse. I was so excited to see her and my family. I didn't sit in on the hearing, but I did find out my grandmother was granted sole custody of me and my dad had visitation rights. Being back in Houston, I ended up going to a new school for the remainder of my elementary school days. It was a Christian private school called Ambassador Christian Academy. Initially I struggled, but the teachers eventually helped me to get caught up academically.

I experienced some form of normalcy being at that school. Every Friday, we got to go out to eat and one year I went on a field trip to San Antonio. I loved that school. One of my most memorable moments would be my teacher reading Frank Peretti's Christian book *This Present Darkness*. That book reminded me of when my mother read the book of Revelations to me in the Bible. Being in that school reignited my love for the Bible and gave me hope things were going to get better in life. I hated leaving that school, but it became too expensive for me to stay. So, I ended up going to another school that was far more different than any other school I had attended.

Tapping into My 'Blackness'

My middle school was within walking distance from my grandmother's house. It was a predominantly black school in Houston's public school system, Albert Thomas Middle School. It was so old all my grandmother's children, including my mother, attended the school. I never knew how I fit in but, having gone to my private school, I excelled academically. Sixth grade was about trying to find the right crowd to fit in with. Seventh grade I began running track, played the clarinet, became a majorette, joined the gospel choir, and got involved with boys.

There were boys in elementary and I had a crush or two but, having been molested, my hormones were raging and nobody at home ever had "the talk" with me. I started talking to different guys and by eighth grade, I was ready to have sex. There were quite a few guys I messed around with and allowed to touch me inappropriately, but I only had sex with one and one time only. The details aren't necessary, but understand it was a very irresponsible act. Some females hated me and some guys only liked me for my looks and what they had heard. I tried to walk around like the gossip didn't bother me, so I put on this façade of being a smart-mouthed bad girl who was ready and willing to curse any person who dared say something stupid to me.

I made it through most of eighth grade with my false confidence until one day a boy who was a well-known drug dealer took my back pack and told me he wouldn't give it back until I gave him oral sex. I was mortified because it was him and three other guys. I boldly said no and threw a few curse words at him, but he would not give me my backpack. Eventually a guy who attended the school's ninth grade academy came out of nowhere and gave me my backpack. He got it back just as my grandmother was coming to pick me up to go to yet another therapy session. I thanked him and got into the car. My grandmother asked what was going on, but I told her nothing. I just sat in the back thinking about how I had been saved by this guy many people were afraid to even talk to. He was like a guardian angel. After that incident, I calmed down. I had a boyfriend and he never once tried to have sex with me. Instead, I began to initiate sexual acts thinking that was the way I needed to be and hoping I would get attention. In the moment, I didn't know it, but I would soon realize I was broken.

Shrinking Back

Towards the end of my eighth-grade year, there was a counselor who knew I performed well academically. She also recognized my bad habits, so she told my grandmother about how I should apply to magnet programs. I applied to quite a few and ended up going to Lamar High School. Lamar was a culture shock for me. It was predominantly white with only a small population of us "hood" kids being bused over every day. I auditioned and made it into the band and that organization became my home for the next four years. Going there shifted something within me. I didn't date any guys, maybe because I never had the opportunity. I was strictly about my books and that kept me focused. I wore baggy clothes and enjoyed being invisible. My ability to be social somewhat diminished. I can definitely say I was not one of the popular girls. Most of them had more money and freedom.

My grandmother was a bit of a stickler, which only made me shut down. I became heavily involved in my church, New Covenant Christian Church, and basically became a role model for the other young girls at the church. I rededicated my life to Christ there and made the commitment to abstain from sex during our Worth the Wait classes. Towards the end of my senior year, I started dating a guy I met while working at the Downtown Aquarium. He was sweet and he honored my vow to not have sex. Even on prom night he respected me, and I'll be forever grateful to him for that. He was a great guy, but we soon went our separate ways. He had one more year left in high school and I was embarking on a new journey…college!

I'm Grown

For college, I ended up attending the University of Houston. College was an interesting time for me. For once, I felt like an adult. I started to go out and with that I connected with boys again. I did join the gospel choir, but that wasn't even enough to keep me disciplined. I was raised seeing people praise God in the church on Sunday and doing every ungodly thing Monday through Saturday; so eventually I succumbed to living a double life. I started coming home really late and one night I came home and my grandmother told me to turn around and leave. I was livid, so I went to stay at my friend's house. That next day, my uncle agreed to help me rent an apartment. I had a roommate and I worked a full-time job while going to school full-time. I ended up picking up some even worse habits and started going out again and having sex. This time it was worse. Some guys were one night stands, while others weren't the only one. In my mind, I thought everything was fine since I was still doing well in school.

Eventually, my irresponsible behavior caught up with me and led to me struggling spiritually, financially, mentally, emotionally, and relationally. Overall, this is the foundation of my journey. There were many more roadblocks but, even through all of this, God managed to teach me numerous lessons. The next few chapters will go more in-depth regarding the process I went through to become free from the bondage that was put on me and the bondage that was self-inflicted.

2

Living a Reality with No Truth

*Make them holy by your truth; teach them your word,
which is truth*
John 17:17 NLT

Reality labeled me as a statistic assuring me I would be nothing more than a woman living a life of promiscuity.
Reality said you were sexually abused so you are used which makes you distasteful to any man.
I WAS convinced my father didn't want me and God took my mommy in an effort to make me walk this earth feeling sad and lonely.
Reality whispered, "You have no significance and your existence is irrelevant, so just be silent for your words are meaningless."
Little did I know, there was a Man who would lay down His life for me and reveal that reality was nothing, but a

hoax created by the enemy to confuse lost individuals like me.

My former pastor from Harvest Time Church preached a sermon focused on our realities versus truth. The synopsis was that we often accept what we see in the natural as our reality. We build our whole life based upon what occurs in the natural. The problem is our reality shouldn't be defined by what we see, instead it should be defined by God's truth. For years, I allowed disappointments to be my reality saying, "Oh well, it is what it is." The problem is that this statement countered God's word and left me in a state of complacency thinking life would never get better. I had experienced an identity crisis that eventually played out through my sexual misconduct.

I'm sure the root of my sexually immoral living was a result of being sexually abused and never saying anything. There were times when I could have spoken up, but I was afraid. I knew if I said anything during the court hearings that incident would have been used to get me to stay with my father. So I stayed silent, not realizing my silence was creating a slow death within me. I soon realized those trips back and forth to Louisiana were very conflicting from life with my grandmother. My father was very liberal and, with me being his only girl, I never believed he knew how to raise me. There was one way we connected and that was through watching movies. Even before he left, we would often watch movies. Unfortunately, the movies my siblings watched were more inappropriate. They included sex scenes which aroused me, but I never said anything about it. Having brothers who would gain control of the TV at night led to me being exposed to pornographic images – and that's where it began. I became fascinated with pornography because it reminded me of what happened when I was molested. I thought it made women appear powerful. In my mind, watching it would be my key to getting a man, keeping him, and pleasing him. There were signs to those who saw my interaction with boys at school, but at home I stayed to myself and was a book worm. I remember being in school, and because boys knew of my bad habits in middle school, they would often refer to me as Diamond from *Playas Club*. That was the future they had established for me and I fed right into that reality as if there was no hope for more. I didn't become a stripper, but I opened myself to many random guys from mutual friends, online, and even the church.

Secret Life

Because I didn't bring my secret lifestyle to church, everyone thought I was living a holy, healthy life. My appearance of being successful was defined by being a college student, not pregnant, actively serving in the church, and being respectful to others. I remember a musician joined my church at the time, and he was a college football player from another state and son of a pastor. So, of course everyone thought we would be a good fit. Unfortunately, he only fed into the problem I was already having. He, too, had a double life, but the only difference was I started being convicted. One thing we don't consider is how familiar spirits link up with each other. I'm sure I didn't really like the guy and he probably didn't really like me, but lust controlled us and caused us to operate out of our flesh. He would have us watching porn and then performing sexual acts from what was seen. It was at that moment I realized I wasn't happy or enjoying it. I was just there because I thought that was what I was supposed to do. Soon I became disgusted and I realized my heart had hardened. I sensed men were taking advantage of me. I never believed they truly cared about me. So I stopped caring about what men wanted and my only goal was to take care of my sexual needs and be done. I thought that would allow me to have some sense of control over my life, but it only left me with more and more holes.

By the time I was in college, I was living with a silent killer. Functioning day to day with a smile on my face, but internally I was damaged. I was angry and the best way to express myself was through cursing, having sex, and being rebellious. All the while, I still went to church and participated in faith-based organizations. I look back and think of how deceitful my life was, but having grown up in the church and seeing so much hypocrisy, I never really knew what living a holy life looked like. The seasoned saints weren't having heart to hearts with me about how to relate with the opposite sex or live a life of holiness. They didn't tell me how to communicate effectively, so I let the world teach me that my reality was the truth.

You see "[i]n the beginning was the Word, and the Word was with God, and the Word was God" (John 1:1 ESV). And the Word became flesh and dwelt among us, and we beheld His glory, the glory as of the only begotten of the Father, full of grace and truth (John 1:14 NKJV). God is the Word and brought it to life through Jesus who was sent full of grace and TRUTH. Reality is an illusion of false truths that leave us feeling defeated. God gave us victory through Jesus Christ (1 Corinthians 15:57); therefore, we should never allow current circumstances or the illusion of defeat to consume us. To differentiate reality and truth we must study God's word. God left us 66 books revealing numerous truths that will silence the realities we have grown to believe as truths. This journey of truth was not completed over night, but overtime I began to see how God aligned the realities of my life to His Truth. Know this, the first step in overcoming is to identify the reality that has plagued your life and then counter it with the Word of God.

3

Learning to Love and Be Loved

Love is patient and kind. Love is not jealous or boastful or proud or rude. It does not demand its own way. It is not irritable, and it keeps no record of being wronged. It does not rejoice about injustice but rejoices whenever the truth wins out. Love never gives up, never loses faith, is always hopeful, and endures through every circumstance.
1 Corinthians 13:4-7 NLT

Released from the womb with an abundance of love
Received from all directions having no understanding of what was to come.
Entering a world where the majority distorts it while the minority reclaim and sustain it.

It was intended to be Unconditional, Kind, Patient, True and Unaffiliated with anything evil,

But there came a time when the enemy MANIPULATED its meaning causing many of us to forget what love really means.

Abandonment, Addiction, and Abuse was the trinity that created a misconception of what love is.
Thoughts of confusion begin to cloud the mind and harden your heart causing you to search for love in all the wrong places.
Leading you into a world of self-destruction.

It's not until one silent moment of your chaotic life, you hear the Lord LOUD and CLEAR as he whispers in your ear, "I LOVE YOU."
The sound of that voice sounds so familiar causing the shell over your heart to crack.

Seeing you're still not convinced He sends a laborer or two WHO intervene and show you what it LOOKS LIKE to be loved by Him.
They care for you and ask about your well- being.
They don't condemn or lie to you. They simply just pray and remind you of WHO God is.
A piece of the shell begins to fall and soon you begin to reminisce about the love you once had as a child.
Remembering the security, peace, and confidence you had, knowing He was always there.

Drawn into His presence, you enter His house surrounded by His love and those who've reclaimed and sustained it.

In AWE of the abundance of love you WEEP to the altar having shells fall with every tear until your heart is softened.
Your life flashes before your eyes and you finally realize this love you thought you had lost, had NEVER left at all. His love is what kept you in the midst of the enemy's attempts to make you forget it ever existed.

With a renewed mind and better understanding, you begin to heal. Allowing God to be the greatest love you've ever known.
This revelation FILLS your holes and STRENGTHENS your heart to where now YOU are the laborer spreading the good news about…. the abundance of HIS love.

After being molested and feeling pretty much invisible, I spent years living a secret life of promiscuity. Pornography was like a drug and if I allowed my flesh to get the best of me, it was a quick fix. I saw no value in my life. I didn't have an outlet, so I wore a mask that allowed me to appear as if everything was alright when in actuality I was broken inside. I would sleep with guys seeking value, only to find out I was nothing more than a temporary fix or an option. At that time, if there was a man who genuinely loved me I didn't recognize it and the ones I thought I loved were battling the same demons I was.

There came a time when I was diagnosed with a series of sexually transmitted diseases such as gonorrhea, chlamydia, and the human papillomavirus (HPV). Gonorrhea and chlamydia didn't scare me, but hearing I had contracted an incurable disease left me in a state of depression. I didn't ask God why because in my mind I deserved it. I was living a double life and because I thought I could run my life, I embraced a reality that I wouldn't get married or have kids. I continued to go to church and I listened to the sermons, but I had yet to experience God's love. Despite that, I got to a point where I felt like I owed God. For three years I spent time reconnecting with Christ. I repented and began to read His Word and mentally prepared myself to live my life as a nun. It wasn't until I went to the doctor for my annual well-woman's exam and my doctor asked me if I needed any contraceptives that everything changed. My response was, "For what, I'm not trying to spread this infection." My doctor then informed me that whatever trace of HPV I had was gone. I was in a state of shock and as unemotional as I appeared to be in person, I went in my car and cried out to God thanking Him for healing me. It was at that moment when I heard the Lord say, "I love you and I will never forsake you."

God's love was the only cure to my life of promiscuity. I realized I couldn't receive nor give love because I had yet to gain a true understanding of the One who is love…God! 1 John 4:8 states, "Anyone who does not love does not know God, because God is love." I couldn't love myself nor anyone else because I had not experienced the love of God. My greatest encounter with God's love manifested when I came to know Him as my healer. God often gives an experience to those who struggle to believe Him the most. It's like two extremes must experience God to believe, the unbeliever who is skeptical and the religious believer whose ability to believe is clouded by false doctrine and religion. I was a religious believer who knew all the do's and don'ts of Christianity, but I did not understand how to apply it. From that moment on, God began to heal more areas of my life.

Forgiveness

As previously mentioned, my father committed adultery and left me and my mother. After my mother's death, my father wasted no time marrying the woman he left us for. He never consulted me or considered focusing on his kids. Instead, he began caring for my step-mother and her kids. I eventually had to spend holidays in Louisiana with him and his new family, but I never could fully accept everyone. My brothers appeared to be coping well, but I was the only one who had lost my mother and I was the only one who didn't have other siblings from my mom.

Although I was physically healed, I lacked respect for men. Most of the men in my family were very selfish and prideful. My brothers were in and out of jail and they did not know how to love. I was no longer being sexually immoral, but I wasn't honoring my father or operating in love. Sometimes we gain one victory as if it makes us better, but the truth is we are all a work in progress and we must surrender every aspect of our life. My relationship with my father was very significant to my growth. Because of what he had done, I was angry. I had a smart mouth and I would always throw his past failures in his face. For me, I just wanted him to acknowledge the wrong he did and to put me before his wife and step-children. To some that may be common sense, but the more I found out about my family's history, the more I understood why my father didn't love well. He loved the best way he knew how to love.

My father's father had a history of not staying committed to the family as well. According to my father, my grandfather had my father and two other sons with my grandmother. Then, while fighting in the military overseas he had two daughters with a French woman who we never met. When he came back, he remarried my grandmother's first cousin and had another five kids. Hearing this helped me to realize the impact of generational patterns. Nonetheless, God used my father to teach me what true forgiveness looked like. At some point in my father's life, he started to get sick. He said it was an extreme case of asthma, but I always felt like it was guilt and shame. The older I got, the more I realized my dad was carrying a burden with his new family. He tried to be the breadwinner and make up for not being a good father to his own by trying to be everything for his step-children and their children. When my father moved back to Louisiana, he was living off of disability so he took a job working a paper route. He loved the country life, but it definitely came at the cost of struggling financially.

As time passed, my dad started moving slower. He then started becoming very apologetic for the mistakes he had made. He even called my maternal grandmother and thanked her for raising me. He recommitted his life back to Christ and started getting back in the Word of God. He also started writing daily devotionals. I was skeptical at first because trust was not an easy thing for me to do, but as God continued to work within me, He helped me to realize my father truly was changing. My father called me pretty much every day and we would talk about God, life, and how proud he was of his baby girl. Eventually, God reconciled our relationship. I realized I only had one father and he was making every effort to right the wrongs he had done. The more I grew spiritually, the better my relationship with my father had gotten. I forgave him knowing that forgiving him was not only going to bring healing to him, but it would also heal me.

Around 2013 things began to shift drastically. Within a year my dad's older brothers and he died in their exact birth order. The night before my dad died he had sent his devotional as usual. On August 30, 2014, I was coming out of a movie theater. I got in the car and saw missed calls from my dad's phone and my step-mom. My step-mom had left a message saying call her back, so I did. She answered and said "Ashlei your daddy is gone". The news sent me back to the day my mom had died. My step mother said they were at a therapy session for my step-sister's daughter. She said my father went to the restroom and he was in there for a while, so she asked someone to check on him. The door was locked so someone got a key and when they opened the door they found him lying on the ground dead. Because of the many problems my dad had with asthma, most people thought that would be cause of his death, but instead a heart attack is what took his life. After being in shock, I cried. My first thoughts were the fact that he wouldn't be there for the most significant moments of my life, such as graduating with my doctoral degree, getting a house, getting married, traveling the world, and having children. All of those dreams seemed like they were gone in the blink of an eye.

By this time, both of my brothers were out of jail so they were able to be at the funeral. I was given the opportunity to speak. While at the funeral I cried, but I was also relieved because I knew my dad had recommitted his life to Christ. I knew he was going to be in Heaven. Knowing this is what gave me the strength to speak at my father's funeral. I don't recall everything I said, but the pastor and friends said it was a word for many. I reread my father's last message because within his words I could tell he knew his time was drawing near. I was at peace with my father's death. There were many nights I cried just thinking about him being gone and even now I get a little teary eyed, but the Lord always reminds me I will see my father again. In spite of the wrongs my father did, I can honestly say he taught me to forgive and to believe deliverance and transformation in an individual's heart is available to all. Every time I felt wronged or when I condemned myself for doing things that were wrong, I thought of my father and I was quick to forgive. God used my father to show me people could change.

I forgave my cousin who molested me. Christmas, I gave everyone on my mom's side of the family a faith-based book and wrote them encouraging letters. I gave my cousin the book *Unqualified* by Steven Furtick and I told him I believe people can change through Christ and I had forgiven him. I let him know I would be speaking up against interfamilial molestation because it's an abuse that is often hidden, crippling so many people. He never apologized, but he did say thank you via social media.

Orphan

After my father's death I almost went into a state of depression feeling as if I was all alone. My brothers were married with children, and I was still single with a family on both sides who did not communicate with me often. Although my grandmother raised me, we always had tension in our relationship. When she started raising me, I always felt like there was some level of bitterness towards me because her husband died, four months later my mother died, and then she retired and raised me. I never felt the perks of being a grandchild. Instead I felt like a replacement child who could never do anything right. I think that was the hardest part with losing my father, because he was very loving and he wasn't afraid to say it. I can't recall my grandmother ever saying I love you as a child. Like all things, her lack of affection was tied to her own past that I have yet to fully know. I used to ask questions, but with enough push back you eventually just let it rest. Don't get me wrong she wasn't heartless, but there were many put downs spoken towards me that made helping me financially or taking care of me seem more like a burden than a blessing. When I was younger it infuriated me, but as I matured in my faith God showed me how to love beyond mistreatment. I can definitely see my prayers have been availing as our relationship continues to grow healthier, slowly but surely.

My biological family may not have been the most affectionate, but God positioned amazing people in my life through church members and a women's ministry called Glittering Sword. There was much freedom that came with fellowshipping with believers. They became my family and with them I began to heal from feeling abandoned. It was through community that I once again was touched by the love of God. My perspective on life began to shift and soon my focus was geared towards fulfilling the purpose God placed on my life.

I had to learn my worth and value will never be dependent upon people and that it had already defined by Christ. No individual has the power to increase or decrease our worth and value, so I had to stop allowing an individual's lack of attention towards me to make me feel and act as if I was nothing. In Christ, we are everything, and another person's inability to see that reflects their lack of identity and not ours. Psalms 139: 13-18 NLT states,

You made all the delicate, inner parts of my body and knit me together in my mother's womb. Thank you for making me so wonderfully complex! Your workmanship is marvelous—how well I know it. You watched me as I was being formed in utter seclusion, as I was woven together in the dark of the womb. You saw me before I was born.

Every day of my life was recorded in your book. Every moment was laid out before a single day had passed. How precious are your thoughts about me, O God. They cannot be numbered! I can't even count them; they outnumber the grains of sand! And when I wake up, you are still with me!

Remember God was very intentional when He created us. He invested His best into us and didn't do it as an afterthought. Once I embraced this truth, I could move forward and begin to understand what He created me to do.

4

Reason for Being

*The Spirit of the Lord God is upon me,
Because the Lord has anointed and commissioned me To
bring good news to the humble and afflicted;
He has sent me to bind up [the wounds of] the
brokenhearted, To proclaim release [from confinement
and condemnation] to the [physical and spiritual]
captives and freedom to prisoners,
To proclaim the favorable year of the Lord,
And the day of vengeance and retribution of our God,
To comfort all who mourn,
To grant to those who mourn in Zion the following:
To give them a turban instead of dust [on their heads, a
sign of mourning],
The oil of joy instead of mourning,
The garment [expressive] of praise instead of a
disheartened spirit. So they will be called the trees of
righteousness [strong and magnificent, distinguished for
integrity, justice, and right standing with God],*

The planting of the Lord, that He may be glorified.
Isaiah 61:1-3 AMP

I knew I had a life to live
Created for something greater than my current position
Those before me were gone
So redemption of my legacy fell on me
Feeling as destined yet rejected as Joseph
As pregnant with hope as Mary
God always reminded me I had a destiny
Who, What, When, Where, Why, and How
Questions often flood my mind
I have yet to receive all the answers
But I know now's the time to understand and walk in my purpose.

My father's death paved the way for me to really focus on what God had left me to do in life. As mentioned in the last chapter, my perspective shifted to where I valued my life more than ever. I was no longer just living for myself, but I was living for my children and their children. While on my lunch break at my accounts payable job years before my father's death, I remember going to a T-Mobile store and leaving with a receipt that had Jeremiah 29:11 and Psalm 37:4 written on it. It caught me by surprise because T-Mobile is not a Christian-based establishment. I rushed back to my cubicle to find out what the verses meant.

For I know the plans and thoughts that I have for you,'
says the LORD, 'plans for peace and well-being and not

> *for disaster, to give you a future and a hope.*
> *Jeremiah 29:11 AMP*

> *Delight yourself in the LORD,*
> *And He will give you the desires and petitions of your heart.*
> *Psalm 37:4 AMP*

In my mind, these verses were God's way of saying there is more in store for me. They served as friendly reminders that any challenges faced were not always going to be that way. They also gave me the hope that I needed as I pursued purpose.

God always had a funny way of speaking to me. He didn't speak with a loud boisterous voice, He spoke to me through words whether it was a sign, conversation, or even a person. I remember when I was in the process of completing a School of Ministry program at my church at the time. While in the School of Ministry class, I was assigned to meditate on purpose. I had always known God had something amazing in store for me, but I didn't have much clarity on how that looked. I struggled to verbalize it. I was told to consider what I love to do. At the time, I was a teacher. In my mind, I thought I would just be teaching, but one thing an Elder told me during my program was my purpose is progressive. Hearing that challenged me to think beyond just being a teacher. Prior to discussing my purpose with the Pastor over the School of Ministry, I went to a women's retreat where God spoke through a woman who gave me a prophetic word based upon Isaiah 61:1-3.

I meditated on this scripture for hours because it resonated with me so much. I examined my life and I heard the words embrace, educate, and empower. I sat silently and then I heard embrace the brokenhearted, educate the lost, and empower the hopeless. As soon as I wrote it in my journal, I turned to a friend of mine with excitement saying this is it. This is what I am called to do. In all my joy, I went to the meeting with the Pastor and was told that was too long. She said I was called to teach. I wrestled with that because I knew I was called to do more than that. After the revelation of my purpose, I started really taking time out to assess how what I was doing in life aligned with that purpose. More flashbacks started coming to me regarding my past and how I was brokenhearted, lost, and hopeless. Then I reflected on the type of people I would encounter whether it be at work or church. Soon it became obvious that God had used my whole life to prepare me to walk in purpose. I began to think about how He used me and realized it was through education.

Preparation

During grade school, I had always been somewhat of a book nerd. I loved to read and write. I had a wild imagination and I dreamed of traveling the world. I used to research places in the encyclopedia, the actual books, and via Brittanica Online. I was very studious and even when I was living a promiscuous life, the one consistent area of my life was my performance in school. I wasn't a genius, but I loved to study. In high school, I had a few teachers who would assign me to help students who I later found out had learning disabilities. Even in band I was an instructor, being the Captain of the color guard team and then being hired the year after I graduated to be the girls' director. As far as writing, I loved English because it gave me the opportunity to read and create. I journaled often as an outlet when I got into middle school.

By the time I entered college at the University of Houston, I knew I wanted to be a teacher and I wanted to specialize in English, so I majored in English and minored in Teacher Education. I did well in my program considering I worked full-time. Unfortunately, I hit a roadblock during my junior year when I had to change my minor due to not being able to student teach, which would require me to stop working. So, I changed my major to Business Administration. By far one of the worst educational decisions I have ever made. Thankfully, the Lord allowed me to graduate.

Upon graduation, I still had the urge to teach, so I applied for a Master's program at my same university and that process was an act of God himself. I applied about one month before the deadline. I had to rush and take the GRE and I failed miserably scoring a 700. Amazingly enough, I was conditionally accepted into their Curriculum & Instruction program. After the first year, I had a GPA of 4.0, so my conditional status was removed. Once again, I excelled in the program and the final year arrived requiring me to student teach. By this time, my faith level was a lot higher. I wasn't wealthy and my father had not contributed anything towards my education, so I was learning off loans. Because my father took money out of his pension early, I no longer qualified for financial aid even though my grandmother was technically my guardian. I know many are against loans, but in my case God said go! I ended up student teaching 4th and 5th grade, but I was certified to teach grades 4-8.

After a semester of student teaching, I completed my comp exams and graduated. As soon as I graduated, the race to find a teaching job was on. I struggled to find a job until one of the pastors at my church told me to apply for the charter school that was opening the following year. I was nervous considering I would be teaching elementary. I figured I have nothing to lose, so I applied, interviewed, and got the job! I will admit working for a first-year charter school was challenging, yet rewarding. I ended up teaching 2nd and 3rd grade English Language Arts & Reading combined.

As a teacher, I put in many long hours to ensure my students were getting the best out of me. What I loved the most was seeing how knowledgeable the kids were of the Bible. I had one student who rarely paid attention to read alouds or independent reading, but when he had a Children's Bible he was always engaged. By the end of that year, I was ready to transition so I applied to work in Houston Independent School District (ISD) which is the largest school district in the Houston, TX area. I will admit I did not apply the listening side of praying when considering what school to choose. I said yes to the first school that offered me a job and it was a horrible mistake. I saw financial increase and ran with it. By October of that same year, I was the seventh teacher to resign. That was my first experience with a mega district and it was a political beast. There was so much corruption from leadership that it made me want to leave education altogether.

Upon leaving, I applied for one reading intervention position in Humble ISD and for a flight attendant position. The last day working in Houston ISD, I received a call to interview in Humble ISD. On the day I interviewed to become a flight attendant, I was offered the job at a middle school in Humble ISD. Just like that, God managed to reel me back into education. I worked with that school as an interventionist for the remainder of the year and then became a contract teacher for the next two years. Once again, God allowed me to speak life into my students and coworkers. He showed me how to be the light even in the midst of working with challenging adults. While there, God told me to move forward on getting my doctoral degree.

I initially was accepted to an online Educational Leadership doctoral degree, but this time God said no. I struggled with the idea of going back to school because I didn't even know if I loved education enough. I eventually did some research and came across Sam Houston State University's Literacy program. The dean at the time was amazing. She had a conversation with me and asked me to send my letter of intent. This was when God began to show me how he had been preparing me all along. Back when I was completing my masters, I wrote a research paper on using the Bible as Literature. It was about 10 pages long and I wrote it in one day. Yes, God was all over that! I ended up making an A+. Well, when I wrote my letter of intent for my doctoral degree, the Lord told me to focus on

Biblical literacy. The dean at the university mentioned how unique that was and immediately told me to submit the required admission documents and in less than a month I was accepted. I continued to teach full-time, and I received a few scholarships, but once again I had to use loans. I did not want to because I knew the stigma with getting loans, but God reminded me once again He would supply all my needs (Philippians 4:19).

While still completing my doctoral degree, I was hired to work in Katy ISD at a more affluent school. Again God highlighted those individuals who He needed to be encouraged and those who would serve as encouragement for me. Working there was a nice change. There were problems, but nothing too extreme. The administration was phenomenal and my team members were very supportive. I worked there two years and then God began to tug at my heart once again regarding my role in education. It was time to move to the next level, but I knew becoming an administrator was not the direction I wanted to go. I needed to be with the students and teachers, so God sent me back full circle to the place that almost made me quit education- Houston ISD. I interviewed for a Teacher Development Specialist position and God showed me tremendous favor.

I was the youngest and had the least classroom experience, but the wisdom of the Lord gave me the skills, words, and strategies to do things that most with my experience would not have known to do. I ended up working at one of the lowest performing middle schools and just as before, the leadership was corrupt. I was attacked on so many levels from being lied on, talked about, disrespected, forced to do jobs that did not align with my job description, etc. There were many nights I cried because I was filled with a righteous anger. The students were treated so poorly and many of the teachers were no better. God always reminded me it was a spiritual battle, so I had to always say to myself that "[I was] not fighting against flesh-and-blood enemies, but against evil rulers and authorities of the unseen world, against mighty powers in this dark world, and against evil spirits in the heavenly places" (Ephesians 6:12).

My ability to love unconditionally was tested. December of that school year, I graduated with my doctoral degree and there were many who did not want to acknowledge my accomplishment. I literally could see leaders and some teachers cringe at the thought of calling me Dr. Evans. I didn't require it, but envy is real. Working at that campus made me feel like Daniel in the lions' den. I never received apologies or anything, but God showed me his faithfulness. When I finished working on that campus, I felt a weight being lifted. Those who were for me were grateful and those who were not for me, I took them to the altar and wished them well.

As much of a journey as this had been, I realized God had me operating in my purpose all along. Every aspect of my life trained me and challenged me to be stretched so I could be used on a greater level. When I think of my calling and how strategic God can be when preparing us, I'm led to Moses. Moses was born a Levite (Hebrew), and at the time Pharaoh had ordered all Hebrew sons be cast into the Nile and killed. Moses was sent down the river in a basket and found by Pharaoh's daughter. He was then taken into the royal house of Egyptians and raised as an Egyptian (Exodus 2). After an incident where Moses kills an Egyptian guard for beating a Hebrew slave, Moses runs away and enters his wilderness season. It wasn't until years later that God finally tells Moses he must go back to Egypt and deliver Israel (Exodus 3:7-10).

Then the LORD told him, "I have certainly seen the oppression of my people in Egypt. I have heard their cries of distress because of their harsh slave drivers. Yes, I am aware of their suffering. So I have come down to rescue them from the power of the Egyptians and lead them out of Egypt into their own fertile and spacious land. It is a land flowing with milk and honey—the land where the Canaanites, Hittites, Amorites, Perizzites, Hivites, and Jebusites now live. Look! The cry of the people of Israel has reached me, and I have seen how harshly the Egyptians abuse them. Now go, for I am sending you to Pharaoh. You must lead my people Israel out of Egypt."
Exodus 3:7-10 NLT

Moses had been called to where he had already been, and many times that is how God operates with us. You may have been abused or struggled with an addiction and you always seemed to find yourself ministering to people who were struggling with what you went through. You may feel like you aren't ready, but Moses felt the same way and for every question of doubt God had an answer of hope for Moses (Exodus 3:11-21 NLT).

But Moses protested to God, "Who am I to appear before Pharaoh? Who am I to lead the people of Israel out of Egypt?"

God answered, "I will be with you. And this is your sign that I am the one who has sent you: When you have brought the people out of Egypt, you will worship God at this very mountain." But Moses protested, "If I go to the people of Israel and tell them, 'The God of your ancestors has sent me to you,' they will ask me, 'What is his name?' Then what should I tell them?" God replied to Moses, "I AM WHO I AM. Say this to the people of Israel: I AM has sent me to you." God also said to Moses, "Say this to the people of Israel: Yahweh, the God of your ancestors—the God of Abraham, the God of Isaac, and the God of Jacob—has sent me to you. This is my eternal name, my name to remember for all generations.

"Now go and call together all the elders of Israel. Tell them, 'Yahweh, the God of your ancestors—the God of Abraham, Isaac, and Jacob—has appeared to me. He told me, "I have been watching closely, and I see how the Egyptians are treating you. I have promised to rescue you from your oppression in Egypt. I will lead you to a land flowing with milk and honey—the land where the Canaanites, Hittites, Amorites, Perizzites, Hivites, and Jebusites now live." ' "The elders of Israel will accept your message. Then you and the elders must go to the king of Egypt and tell him, 'The LORD, the God of the Hebrews, has met with us. So please let us take a three-day journey into the wilderness to offer sacrifices to the LORD, our God.'

> *"But I know that the king of Egypt will not let you go unless a mighty hand forces him. So I will raise my hand and strike the Egyptians, performing all kinds of miracles among them. Then at last he will let you go. And I will cause the Egyptians to look favorably on you. They will give you gifts when you go so you will not leave empty-handed.*
> *Exodus 3:11-21 NLT*

God's greatest response was He is the great I Am! Because we serve the I Am who can do all things we have no need to worry about what we can and cannot do in our natural state.

I encourage you to seek God and ask Him to reveal your calling. Ask Him to open your eyes, ears, mind, and heart so you may become more aware of Him operating through you as you go through your day. Remember, like Moses, there is a group of people God has called us to deliver. Whether it be in arts & entertainment, the government, business, education, media, or religion, there is a group of people waiting for their Moses to help lead them out of their Egypt.

5

Trusting the Position and the Process

Don't let anyone look down on you because you are young, but set an example for the believers in speech, in conduct, in love, in faith and in purity.
1 Timothy 4:12 NIV

Youthful looking I may be,
But power lies within the words inside of me
Don't neglect what God has given me,
Because you may miss the blessing He wants to give you through me.

My demeanor should not intimidate you,
I am simply living as the example God intended me to be for you.
Don't let my faith seem outlandish,
I am only believing and fully depending on what God has promised me.

Where I am today is not where I was yesterday,
And it is where I won't be come tomorrow.
Don't allow my current state to fool you into thinking I can't relate,
For my past is what has allowed me to be a present example to you and hope of what you can become in the future.

After gaining a sense of identity and purpose, I would often question my ability to really be greater than the person I was seeing. I was crippled by fear and I would box myself in to thinking there was only one way to be used to draw people into the Kingdom of God. What I failed to realize is that the way I reached people was going to be different, because the life I lived was strategically planned so I would be able to reach a specific audience. My mind began to expand after attending the *One Thing* conference held in Kansas City, Missouri. It was hosted by the International House of Prayer. It was there I came to the knowledge of how God would use me prophetically through writing and speaking. Going to that conference unlocked a new level of thinking for me.

I began studying The Word more intentionally and my relationship with God grew stronger. I recall one time I went on a 30-day fast and I just meditated on 1 Kings 3:7-10 when King Solomon asked God for wisdom. Then I read through Proverbs. I've never forgotten that fast because I really wanted to have wisdom. I knew the mistakes I had made in the past, and I was determined to do better in every aspect of my life. I wanted to do things God's way.

There are many times people are discounted because of their looks, marital status, abilities, societal status, income, education, and age. It's almost as if wisdom has been labeled as being given to only a certain type of person. Wisdom is not a respecter of persons and the release of it is not limited to experience or age. It is given to those who will use it to bring glory to God. It is a gift given by God to be used to bring people back to Him. What's amazing is all you have to do on your part is ask and believe you've received it. After that fast, my faith increased tremendously, but I soon found I would get stuck trusting God during the waiting process.

God had given me so many prophetic utterances directly and through people. Upon hearing them, I realized I have much faith that God will do something great with my life. However, in the waiting, I began to question whether or not I was trusting Him to lead me to the promise He gave. I had faith that God would fulfill His end of the covenant, but sometimes I did not trust the way He desired to get me there. For instance, God gave me a list of places that I would travel including Washington D.C., London, and South Africa. An opportunity came for Glittering Sword, the women's ministry I served with, to lead worship at David's Tent in Washington D.C., which held prayer for our Nation. Initially lack of finances were always the reason I was not able to travel, but this time I decreed and declared it and I made it there. Next, a church I was attending for a short period of time was planning a mission trip to South Africa. I had two weeks to raise the money for the trip, and I was never a good fundraiser. The Pastor asked me if I wanted to go because someone dropped out, and speaking out of faith I said yes. Within two weeks, family, friends, coworkers, and church members sowed into the trip. I later found out we had a seven-hour layover in London, so I was able to go out and walk through London. This was all an act of God! In my mind I thought I would go to these places for a vacation, but God always sent me for ministry and in the process I was blessed as well.

When I think about the battle between faith and trust, I think about Abram and Sarai. In Genesis 15, God tells Abram he will have his own heir.

But Abram replied, "O Sovereign LORD, what good are all your blessings when I don't even have a son? Since you've given me no children, Eliezer of Damascus, a servant in my household, will inherit all my wealth. You have given me no descendants of my own, so one of my servants will be my heir."

Then the LORD said to him, "No, your servant will not be your heir, for you will have a son of your own who will be your heir." Then the LORD took Abram outside and said to him, "Look up into the sky and count the stars if you can. That's how many descendants you will have!"

And Abram believed the LORD, and the LORD counted him as righteous because of his faith.

Genesis 15:2-6 NLT

Even after being told he would have his own son, Abram and Sarai found themselves not trusting God's process. I say Abram AND Sarai, because Abram's next act reveals somewhere in his heart he too believed God had left him to bear a child on his own. In Genesis 16, we find Sarai reflecting on her barrenness. Instead of reaching out to God and trusting Him to fulfill the promise He gave Abram, she tells Abram to sleep with their servant Hagar who ultimately bears a son.

Upon the birth of Hagar and Abram's son Ishmael, God revisits Abram and reestablishes His covenant with him and Sarai as Abraham and Sarah. During this visit, God tells Abraham that Sarah will bear him a son named, Isaac.

And I will bless her and give you a son from her! Yes, I will bless her richly, and she will become the mother of many nations. Kings of nations will be among her descendants."
Then Abraham bowed down to the ground, but he laughed to himself in disbelief. "How could I become a father at the age of 100?" he thought. "And how can Sarah have a baby when she is ninety years old?" So Abraham said to God, "May Ishmael live under your special blessing!" But God replied, "No—Sarah, your wife, will give birth to a son for you. You will name him Isaac, and I will confirm my covenant with him and his descendants as an everlasting covenant. As for Ishmael, I will bless him also, just as you have asked. I will make him extremely fruitful and multiply his descendants. He will become the father of twelve princes, and I will make him a great nation. But my covenant will be confirmed with Isaac, who will be born to you and Sarah about this time next year."
Genesis 17:16-21 NLT

God previously told Abraham he would have his own heir, but he did not trust God to bring the promise into fruition. How many times have we moved out of fear as if we have the ability to help God manifest the promise He gave? If you don't want to be honest, I'll raise my hand…both of them. I didn't have all the details, so I failed to trust God would deliver in HIS way and HIS timing. My lack of trust didn't cancel the promise, but it did delay a few things.

Trust in the Lord with all your heart,
and do not lean on your own understanding.
In all your ways acknowledge him,
and he will make straight your paths.
Proverbs 3:5-6 ESV

Proverbs 3:5-6 tells us if we trust God beyond our human minds, He will guide our paths. By trusting God, we receive divine direction. He orders our steps and leads us to the right people and places needed to fulfill His promise.

Because of what we've seen God do, our faith grows strong, but when the process begins to differ, we lack trust. I challenge you to no longer try to reach the destination God has for you out of your own might. Instead, trust and believe He has already created the steps He has for you to get there. Silence your thoughts, worship Him, read His Word, and listen for instruction. Psalm 32:8 reminds us that God will instruct us and teach us in the way we should go. He will counsel us with His eye upon us. No matter what detours and trials we may experience or what the promise or assignment given to us may be, we must maintain our trust in God knowing He is too faithful for us to not trust Him.

6

Running the Race

Each time he said, "My grace is all you need. My power works best in weakness." So now I am glad to boast about my weaknesses, so that the power of Christ can work through me.
2 Corinthians 12:9 NLT

Like Jesus I asked if this cup of suffering could be taken away from me
The pain became unbearable
Making me not want to bear any burden at all
I was ready to quit
But you just wouldn't let me
Every time I fell you held out your hand to help me
You said, "This cup is greater than just My being
Just like Jesus it will save lives by introducing the lost to Me."
Understanding this race is bigger than me, I surrendered like Mary and said
"Lord let it be to me according to your Word"

As I continued my journey with Christ, I would have seasons where I felt like everything was going well and then there were seasons where I felt like all hell had broken loose. I would experience a heaviness that would make me contemplate all I was doing. I had many moments of weakness that revealed another layer of healing needed to take place in my life. There were times when I failed maintaining my purity and overall being disobedient through thought, action, or speech. I was often overlooked and hurt by many people to the point that I would cry out to God wondering why I had to suffer. Even in those moments, God turned me to His Word and reminded me there was at least one person who had experienced something similar or worse. This gave me the strength and hope to persevere.

Esther, David, Joseph, Moses, Daniel, and so many others were all underestimated, overlooked, disrespected, and considered to be 'less than' by man. Yet God raised them up among earthly Kings and Queens and positioned them to have influence to take the throne as royal heirs of God's Kingdom. Job 8:7 declares "though your beginning was small, your latter days will be great." Knowing this and understanding God's Word is truth challenged me to never forget my royal lineage. As noted in former chapters, I didn't come from the ideal family. We weren't wealthy and dysfunction exists on both sides. In spite of my situations, I had to claim my position on the throne and that came with confessing the Word of God and seeing myself through the eyes of God. I could not be moved by what I didn't see in the natural, I had to move based upon the promises God revealed to me. Anytime I felt overlooked or forgotten I would confess 1 Peter 2:9 ESV over myself, "But you are a chosen race, a royal priesthood, a holy nation, a people for his own possession, that you may proclaim the excellencies of him who called you out of darkness into his marvelous light."

Another struggle I faced was being hidden. These were times when I knew I had much to offer, but it seemed like I never got the chance to operate in my gifting. What I came to realize was being hidden was not a sign of being neglected or rejected. It was an opportunity to develop, grow, and be prepared to be exposed in a more mature state. In this place there was a special covering and level of protection from those things sent to destroy me. For instance, embracing my singleness was hard at times. I would wonder why no one was approaching me. Then there came a time when I would meet a guy and I would fall in sin. Those failures pained me because I wanted to please God, but it revealed healing needed to take place. I would later find out those men were broken and needed healing themselves. I had to thank God for the times he kept me hidden because he had spared me from going through yet another healing process.

Jesus Christ, David, Moses, and Esther are just a few who were all in a hidden state for a season. When they were released, the power of God catapulted through them and touched the lives of many. Whether you are hidden at work, serving at church, within a relationship, or in purpose in general, understand those days of obscurity are to humble and purge us, so when notoriety comes we will stand strong. Your light will shine brighter because you allowed the love of Christ to consume your heart. When feeling hidden just confess Philippians 1:6 knowing God is completing the work he began in you. "**And I am certain that God, who began the good work within you, will continue his work until it is finally finished on the day when Christ Jesus returns.**"

A final struggle I often faced was dealing with pain. The absence of pain is not guaranteed when journeying towards the promise, but I had to rest knowing with pain there is always comfort from the Lord. Pain is a feeling we have all felt whether it was physical or emotional. Nevertheless, we don't like the feeling and oftentimes we question God when He allows us to feel it. I felt this pain when I was molested, when my parents died, and when I was hurt by those I thought cared for me. As pain continued, I learned God will allow the pain if it leads to His will being manifested. But with that, He is also there to bring healing and comfort from the pain. This is shown even with Jesus Christ who went through excruciating pain all in the name of love. I'm sure Jesus didn't like the process, but He understood it had to be done so that the promise of God could be fulfilled. When it all was finished, Christ went on to be with God. He was restored and made whole and that is what God does with us. Our initial reaction to pain is to become angry, but after spending time with God, I've learned to simply say Thank You! The pain is not what we want, but sometimes it's what we need to move forward. When pain begins, allow 2 Corinthians 1:3-7 to minister to your heart.

"All praise to God, the Father of our Lord Jesus Christ. God is our merciful Father and the source of all comfort. He comforts us in all our troubles so that we can comfort others. When they are troubled, we will be able to give them the same comfort God has given us. For the more we suffer for Christ, the more God will shower us with his comfort through Christ. Even when we are weighed down with troubles, it is for your comfort and salvation! For when we ourselves are comforted, we will certainly comfort you. Then you can patiently endure the same things we suffer. We are confident that as you share in our sufferings, you will also share in the comfort God gives us."
2 Corinthians 1:3-7 NLT

God's glory is shown most when we've been in long seasons of testing. So, don't think your struggle is a punishment for something you did or are doing wrong. Instead, consider it a sign God wants to give you a victory greater than your human mind can imagine and greater than what you can do out of your own ability. Remember, we can't have a testimony without a test and if you're like me I want every aspect of my life to be a testimony of God's love and power. Sure enough, every test I've experienced has provided an opportunity for God to show Himself as the loving, omnipotent Father that He is. Going through the test is never easy and there are many times you will question the process, but it leads to you surrendering yourself and the situation to God so that He is finally able to move in and through you.

7

Living a Consecrated Life

Therefore I urge you, brothers and sisters, by the mercies of God, to present your bodies [dedicating all of yourselves, set apart] as a living sacrifice, holy and well-pleasing to God, which is your rational (logical, intelligent) act of worship. And do not be conformed to this world [any longer with its superficial values and customs], but be transformed and progressively changed [as you mature spiritually] by the renewing of your mind [focusing on godly values and ethical attitudes], so that you may prove [for yourselves] what the will of God is, that which is good and acceptable and perfect [in His plan and purpose for you].
Romans 12: 1-2 AMP

Desiring to hear my voice
Hoping that I will reach out to you
Distracted is what I was
Surviving, but not thriving
Emptiness is what I was feeling

Confusion was blocked clarity
Still you stayed by my side
Waiting for me to live a consecrated life

A major component of living a life for Christ is consecrating our life. We do this by choosing to be in relationship with God and walking in holiness. God is too great to be associated with the darkness of this world and, being His children, we too should be committed to living a life that honors God. There was a moment when I realized that I wasn't all in for God like I should have been. I began to feel stagnant, complacent, confused, and empty because my prayer life wasn't consistent and I wasn't being intentional with my walk with God.

Call to Me and I will answer you, and tell you [and even show you] great and mighty things, [things which have been confined and hidden], which you do not know and understand and cannot distinguish.'
Jeremiah 33:3 AMP

I realized I had not been calling out to God. I was not investing my time to communicate and connect with God. We sometimes forget that God enjoys communing with us. He wants to tell us to live our best life and make wise decisions, but we have to be willing to listen. I took a hiatus for 40 days, so I could lean into God and hear Him clearly. Many things were happening in every aspect of my life and spending time with him exposed me to a greater level of peace, joy, wisdom, knowledge, and understanding. During that time, He revealed these 17 nuggets of wisdom that spoke volumes to my life and the many things I had experienced.

1. Happiness was not written in the contract of our salvation.
2. Our joy is not contingent upon what God does for us, but simply for who He is.
3. Sometimes less is more when dealing with friendships. People come and go, but it's not a reflection of who we are, but, more so, of where we're going.
4. Our suffering doesn't mean God has left us. If anything, He's closer than ever so His glory can be seen during our suffering.
5. There's more disunity and judgment within the body than in the world, but those who choose Christ wholeheartedly over being lukewarm will walk in unity and inherit the Kingdom of God. Remember to never allow the use of God's word to cause division in the body. Use it to bring peace through the knowledge of who He is.
6. Every journey is not a straight line, and although it turns into jagged edges, we know the journey is preparing us to walk in the greatness He has for us. Detours come left and right, but if God is at the steering wheel we will be alright.
7. God is faithful and willing and ready to speak to those who will be still and listen. We need to start hearing!

8. Numbers are significant not for quantity, but for the quality. One believer being discipled and walking in the call God has for their lives is far greater than the 100 who said the prayer of salvation and never went into a personal relationship with Christ. Salvation was never meant for us to give a portion of our life to Christ, instead it was to open us up so our life would become His. In this season, the Church should make it our agenda to disciple through the leading of the Holy Spirit.

9. God is love, but He is also just. God's word was never meant to be shared at our convenience. The Word as a whole should be taught because it embodies the fullness of who God is, how He operates, and how He desires to see us move.

10. God moves beyond what the eye can see and oftentimes he's doing it through us in the hidden places of this world. We chase the One rather than trying to be chased by the thousands. Remember all we do is for the glory of God - not ourselves.

11. We must get our priorities straight and be driven by eternity. We don't live our lives for today. Instead, we live for the eternal life already prepared for us in Heaven. Treat life like a video game understanding there are new levels to living a life for Christ every day. Consider every achievement to be the beginning of a new stage in life that will make us stronger and more available to be used by God until we make it to the last round which, in a believer's case, is Heaven.

12. Ministry was never meant to be done alone. For it to flourish, partner first with Christ and those He leads you to. Partnership is the key in this season of ministry.

13. Understand all black churches are not religious, all mega churches are not greedy, and operating in the five-fold is not limited to all white evangelical churches. There are many churches that embody exactly what God desires for His church to be. You must stop chasing popularity and comfort to see these hidden jewels with our spiritual eyes rather than looking through a natural lens.

14. In the matter of marriage, you have not heard God wrong, so we must not beat ourselves up or allow anyone to belittle us because what we saw in the spiritual realm has not manifested in the natural the way we thought it would. God giving freewill to man often leads man to choose permissive will rather than God's perfect will if they are not taking heed to God's voice. Don't settle for anyone less than God's best. Even a good person may not be that great person God desires for us to have. Be still, keep pursuing God's purpose for our life, and wait on the Lord.

15. Embrace every gift God has ever given. We may not be able to use them all in one place, but God will always create time and space for us to grow in our gifts. We just have to keep using them.

16. When we encounter disagreements, respond by taking heed to what the Holy Spirit is saying. It's more about how we handle ourselves than us being right.

17. Living a life of consecration goes beyond occasional fasts and corporate prayer meetings. We must choose to consecrate ourselves daily, by always choosing Christ first in every aspect of our lives. Meditate on the Word of God, worship Him, seek wisdom, ask to be filled with the Holy Spirit, and then listen to Him.

There are many more revelations God has given me, but I choose to stop at 17 because it represents breakthrough and victory. I believe these 17 revelations have drawn me closer to breakthrough in my own life and I'm believing they will do the same for you!

Closing

This means that anyone who belongs to Christ has become a new person. The old life is gone; a new life has begun!
2 Corinthians 5:17 NLT

Many of you who have read this book are at different places in your lives. I wrote this book to share my story in hopes that it would inspire you to receive the love of Christ and embrace who He has created you to be. I will not sell you false dreams that everything in your life will be made perfect, but I will let you know God will do something new in and through you. In spite of all the challenges I've overcome, I know I have not arrived. There is still much growth that must take place, but there is beauty in knowing that God will use me even in my imperfect state. God truly exchanged my ashes for His beauty, and I'm forever grateful. I'm always amazed by how God has transformed my life. I am full of joy and I am clothed with strength and dignity, and [I] laugh without fear of the future. When I speak, my words are wise, and I give instructions with kindness" (Proverbs 31:25-26 NLT).

If you have not given your life to Christ and you are feeling compelled to do so, here is your opportunity. No, you don't have to wait until you go to a church. Romans 10: 9-10 NLT states, "If you openly declare that Jesus is Lord and believe in your heart that God raised him from the dead, you will be saved. For it is by believing in your heart that you are made right with God, and it is by openly declaring your faith that you are saved." Now repeat the prayer below:

Prayer of Salvation

Father God,
I know I am a sinner. I repent of my sins and ask for your forgiveness. I believe you are the Son of God. The one who died for my sins and rose again. Please come into my life and fill me with your Spirit. I receive you as my Lord and Savior Jesus Christ. In Jesus' name I pray, Amen!

Yes! It is that simple. Now, it's best you get connected to a local church that will disciple you and walk with you as you begin to grow in your relationship with God. I leave you with this prayer for spiritual wisdom by the great Apostle Paul.

I pray for you constantly, asking God, the glorious Father of our Lord Jesus Christ, to give you spiritual wisdom and insight so that you might grow in your knowledge of God. I pray that your hearts will be flooded with light so that you can understand the confident hope he has given to those he called—his holy people who are his rich and glorious inheritance. I also pray that you will understand

*the incredible greatness of God's power for us who
believe him. This is the same mighty power that raised
Christ from the dead and seated him in the place of honor
at God's right hand in the heavenly realms. Now he is far
above any ruler or authority or power or leader or
anything else—not only in this world but also in the world
to come. God has put all things under the authority of
Christ and has made him head over all things for the
benefit of the church. And the church is his body; it is
made full and complete by Christ, who fills all things
everywhere with himself.
Ephesians 1:15-23 NLT*

Welcome to The Ash Exchange!

*To all who mourn in Israel
he will give a crown of beauty for ashes,
a joyous blessing instead of mourning,
festive praise instead of despair.
In their righteousness, they will be like great oaks
that the LORD has planted for his own glory.
Isaiah 61:3 NLT*

More from Dr. Ashlei N. Evans

Publications:
Biblical Literacy in a Secular World: Secondary Students' Perceptions of the Influence of Biblical Practices on Academic Achievement

Co-authored projects:
Tying the Knot Between Ministry and the Marketplace Volume 2
Compiler: Deborah D. Taylor

Available Services
Inspirational and motivational speaking (e.g., faith-based, leadership, identity, spiritual gifts)
Life coaching, mentoring, and educational consulting

Connect with this author and speaker for your next event:
Website: www.TheAshExchange.com
Facebook: www.Facebook.com/DrAshleiNEvans
Email: AshleiNEvans@gmail.com or
TheAshExchange@gmail.com

www.ingramcontent.com/pod-product-compliance
Lightning Source LLC
Chambersburg PA
CBHW030915080526
44589CB00010B/314